Z**oom** In on
Stars of Music

Justin Timberlake

Jennifer Strand

abdopublishing.com

Published by Abdo Zoom™, PO Box 398166, Minneapolis, Minnesota 55439. Copyright © 2017 by Abdo Consulting Group, Inc. International copyrights reserved in all countries. No part of this book may be reproduced in any form without written permission from the publisher. Abdo Zoom™ is a trademark and logo of Abdo Consulting Group, Inc.

Printed in the United States of America, North Mankato, Minnesota
102016
012017

**THIS BOOK CONTAINS
RECYCLED MATERIALS**

Cover Photo: Pascal Le Segretain/Getty Images
Interior Photos: Pascal Le Segretain/Getty Images, 1; Shutterstock Images, 4, 6–7; Antonio Scorza/Shutterstock Images, 5; Seth Poppel/Yearbook Library, 7; Everett Collection, 8; Walt Disney Co./Everett Collection, 9; L. Busacca/WireImage/Getty Images, 10; Helle Aasand/The Mississippi Press-Register/AP Images, 11; Schroewig/Jens Koch/Picture-Alliance/DPA/AP Images, 12; Kevork Djansezian/AP Images, 13; Dana Edelson/© 2013 NBCUniversal/Getty Images, 14; Everett Collection/Shutterstock Images, 15; Britta Pedersen/Picture-Alliance/DPA/AP Images, 16–17; Featureflash Photo Agency/Shutterstock Images, 18; Jonathan Pow/PA Wire URN:26280019/AP Images, 18–19

Editor: Emily Temple
Series Designer: Madeline Berger
Art Direction: Dorothy Toth

Publisher's Cataloging-in-Publication Data
Names: Strand, Jennifer, author.
Title: Justin Timberlake / by Jennifer Strand.
Description: Minneapolis, MN : Abdo Zoom, 2017. | Series: Stars of music |
    Includes bibliographical references and index.
Identifiers: LCCN 2016948680 | ISBN 9781680799217 (lib. bdg.) |
    ISBN 9781624025075 (ebook) | 9781624025631 (Read-to-me ebook)
Subjects: LCSH: Timberlake, Justin, 1981- --Juvenile literature. | Rock
    musicians--United States--Biography--Juvenile literature. | Singers--United
    States--Biography--Juvenile literature.
Classification: DDC 782.42164092 [B]--dc23
LC record available at http://lccn.loc.gov/2016948680

Table of Contents

Justin Timberlake is
a singer and actor.

He was first known as a teen music star. Today he is a **popular** entertainer.

Early Life

Justin was born on January 31, 1981. He grew up in Tennessee.

Justin loved music.
He liked to dance and sing.

Justin also loved to perform. He got a part on a TV show. It was called *The All New Mickey Mouse Club.*

He sang, danced, and acted.

Rise to Fame

In 1995 Timberlake helped form a boy band.

It was called *NSYNC. The band released its first album in 1998. Fans were crazy about *NSYNC.

Superstar

Later Timberlake began making music on his own. He released two **solo** albums.

They made him an even bigger star.
He won **Grammy Awards.**

Timberlake also acted. He starred in movies. He also appeared on TV.

He even won an award for
his work on a funny TV show.

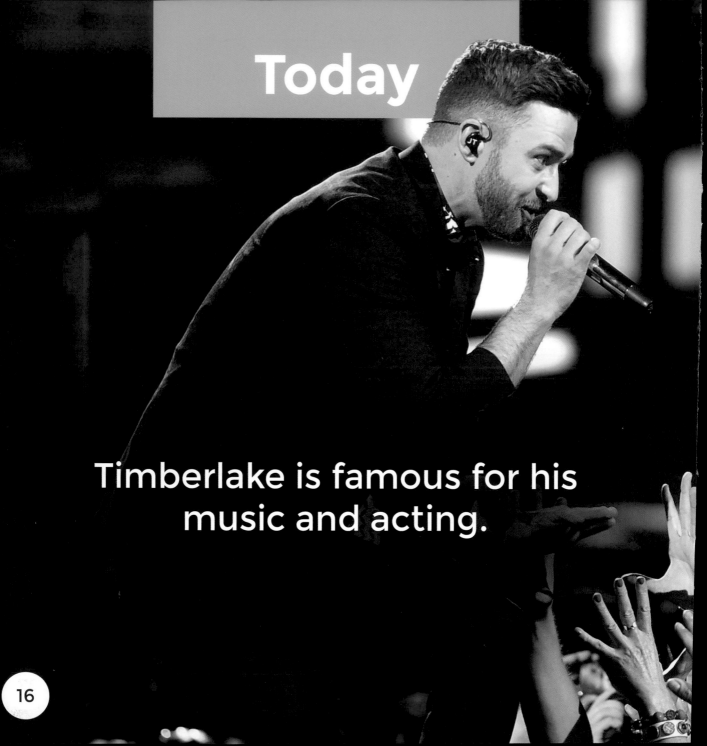

Today

Timberlake is famous for his music and acting.

He also writes music for other singers. He works with many different businesses, too.

In 2016 Timberlake released the song "Can't Stop the Feeling."

It was his fifth number one song as a solo singer. He has fans all over the world.

Justin Timberlake

Born: January 31, 1981

Birthplace: Memphis, Tennessee

Wife: Jessica Biel

Known For: Timberlake is a famous American singer, actor, and entertainer.

Key Dates

1981: Justin Randall Timberlake is born on January 31.

1993: Justin joins *The All New Mickey Mouse Club.*

1998: *NSYNC releases its first album.

2002: Timberlake releases his first solo album.

2009: Timberlake wins an Emmy Award for his work on the TV show *Saturday Night Live.*

2016: "Can't Stop the Feeling" debuts as a number one single.

Glossary

album - a collection of music.

Grammy Award - an important honor given out each year for music. There are many Grammy Awards.

perform - to do something in front of an audience.

popular - liked by many people.

released - made available to the public.

solo - a performance by a single person.

Booklinks

For more information
on **Justin Timberlake**, please visit
booklinks.abdopublishing.com

Zoom In on Biographies!

Learn even more with the Abdo Zoom
Biographies database. Check out
abdozoom.com for more information.

Index